'HELPING STARS'

Easy Guide to Understand Star Sign Incompatibilities and More...

by

Ariane Warren

authorHOUSE™

1663 Liberty Drive, Suite 200
Bloomington, Indiana 47403
(800) 839-8640
www.AuthorHouse.com

First published by AuthorHouse 05/04/05
Rev. 12/04/2012
ISBN: 1-4208-4616-7 (e)
ISBN: 1-4208-4615-9 (sc)

Printed in the United States of America
Bloomington, Indiana

This book is printed on acid-free paper.

Table of Contents

Chapter 1 ★ ★ ★ ★

I NEED TO TELL YOU

The stars that we see in the sky are linked to us. Their vibrations are constantly influencing us, and those that form part of the Zodiac pattern have been known to interact with us from the moment of our birth. It seems as if we are projections of an awesome cosmic formula. Maybe, one day, the legacy of our ancient 'star gazers' may be better understood when our scientific knowledge increases.

Throughout the centuries many have been afflicted by the notion that some Star Signs are incompatible with other Signs. It is for this reason that this booklet is written – to dismiss the notion of incompatibilities by understanding that Star Signs are our 'Helpers' and have the potential to aid us in our daily interpersonal relationships.

Have you ever been told, 'Don't marry him because his Star Sign is incompatible with yours!' – or, 'She is not for you, her Star Sign does not match yours!' How sad some folk have been, and still are, with such a thought… Is there a solution to this predicament?

Not only in our personal life these 'so called' incompatibilities affect us but also in our working relationships. If your Boss is not compatible with you, e.g. he or she may be an Aries and you are a Pisces, you may immediately decide you are going to have a 'big battle' ahead. Well, I can tell you, dear reader, that if you pay attention to what I have to say, you will find your days at work exciting and rewarding, because there are some simple guidelines or, shall we say, 'tools', that can enable you to have some fun working out ways to alleviate incompatibilities.

My booklet is not for the studious astrological researcher – there are ample dissertations on 'Astrology' – and I don't pretend to know the intricacies of such a complicated subject. What I do know is what I learned from a Hungarian Sumerologist, Professor Franz Jos, in the late 60's. He was also an Astrologer, but with a difference! He told me, 'Ariane, I am not like many Astrologers – I follow the Magyar Ancient Star knowledge which primarily offers healing from pain and suffering - by knowing how to utilise the elements we have been given by the Stars to improve our human relationships'.

When I first heard Prof. Jos telling me this, I was a Sunday school teacher – every Sunday afternoon I used to go to his house to collect his grand daughter. When Sunday school was over I would always take his grand daughter back to her home and I would have a cup of tea with him and his wife. After tea, Prof. Jos would show me his research work on Sumerology. This subject fascinated me! However, one day he told me about 'the Stars' (as in The Zodiac). I was so perplexed because, had he not been keen for me to take his grand daughter to Sunday school, and, was it not that Christianity and The Zodiac oppose each other? However, to my surprise, Prof. Jos shook my senses when he told me that The Magi in the Bible were, guess what, yes! Magyars! (He may have meant that the Magyars had originated from these ancient Wise Men). He said that these 'Magyar' astrologers had seen the Star of Bethlehem and had known that Jesus was a human being as 'no other' because his Star formation was unique – they had never seen it before! In the ancient writings they had found the prophesy about his coming!

Wow! I was gob smacked! I could even inaugurate a new phrase: 'I was God smacked!' – how relevant this phrase could be only time will tell.

Many years after, to my astonishment, I saw a new Bible translation with the word 'Astrologers' introduced instead of the well known 'Magi' or 'wise men from the east'. (You may wish to look into this, as I prefer to continue in a casual manner, without references).

Dear reader, please pause for a moment to ponder on my first introduction to astrology – it is very important. Our wonderful stars are not only incredibly beautiful to gaze upon, in the expanse of the heavens – but they are also powerful instruments for our own good – setting a light upon our earthly inner pathway, and even leading us into a knowledge of our 'spiritual' heavenly heritage.

Chapter 2 ★ ★ ★ ★ ★

PERSONAL INSTRUCTIONS
FROM PROF. FRANZ JOS

Many are the advances in science and much about the mystery of the planets is already known to be somewhat related to magnetism and electro-magnetism. Undoubtedly in years to come science will explain fully how planets affect us as individuals.

We already know about the influence of the moon on the tides and many other aspects of earthly life. After all, are not gardeners and farmers acquainted with the sun-moon cycle of growth – and that success or failure will result from an inter dependence with this planetary influence?

As specifically related to us, human beings, would it not seem obvious that we could also be influenced by cosmic energy? Would it be so difficult to imagine that rays of energy or light leave a particular seal or imprint on the moment that we take our first breath of life, and that this could also influence us during our lifetime?

The combination of all this cosmic energy can be observed in plant growth such as the link with 'Water - Fire – Earth - Air' elements akin to what astrologers mention. Hence, some plants are 'water plants' or 'desert plants', some need more or less water, or sun, and so on. If the elements of water, fire, air and earth are directly linked to each and every growing plant, and if these elements are part of our great cosmic totality, why would they not influence us?

Hence we may perhaps agree that we could also share in the notion that we have a particular element that influences our own framework, and that it could affect our very nature.

Today scientists are discovering ways to alter plants...and a great deal more...how about us? Could we learn to adapt and change our planetary blue print? Have the ancient astrologers left us clues to do this? I think so.

Prof. Jos gave me many 'mini' lessons on the greatness of our links with the cosmos. He knew that I would be concerned about choices in life such as 'who would I marry?' and 'how could I be successful with working relationships' and all the perplexing concerns that young folk have when they are entering adulthood.

He emphasized the following points as regarding choosing a partner – the order of the points, he said, was very important. It was surprising to me when the first aspect to consider was not 'which star sign the person was', but, as follows:

1. Find out whether the person is 'positive' or 'negative'
2. How the person was brought up
3. What is their star sign

When he mentioned these points I immediately asked him what he meant by 'a positive or negative person'. He said that I had to listen carefully to a person while they conversed, and if they tended to be negative, for example, if they said, 'Oh what a horrid day I've had...' or 'I hate my boss...' and these negative connotations pervaded their lives, without finding a positive outlook to these daily life experiences then this type of person would not be ideal to enter into any kind of partnership.

The second point also mystified me, and so he explained to me that if a person had been brought up with loving 'positive' parents or carers then this would be a good point to take into consideration.

The third point, which relates to the 'star sign', would only be important if the other two points had been considered first, and not the other way round because sadly enough some folk are often prone to establish a relationship by primarily noting a person's star sign... but incompatibilities would most likely arise if the partner has a negative outlook on life or may have lacked parental role models of love, care and spiritual nourishment during childhood.

The following chapter will further explain this third point, according to my observations throughout the past forty years. However, I feel that mere words cannot express the deeper knowledge that seems to be deposited in our own inner consciousness – in this I mean something similar to the 'homing instinct' that birds and even fish or eels possess to locate their breeding grounds. The wonders of our planetary dependence are awesome – almost incomprehensible – I can only impart an infinitesimal spec of such grandeur.

Chapter 3 ★★★★★

ELEMENTS IN NATURE
AND THE STARS

Prof.Jos told me that when considering a person's star sign the most important aspect of it is its element – whether it was Fire, Earth, Air or Water. The more knowledge one has of these elements the closer one is to understand a person and alleviate incompatibilities.

First of all he told me to look at nature - just to watch a beautiful landscape. While observing the horizon it would seem that the earth and sky do not mix – that there is a demarcation between earth and sky. The earth is firm and secure under our feet and a clear distinction appears to separate the earth and the sky. We feel that the earth is firm, strong and predictable but the sky is so different… mysterious, magnificent and daunting. Even though we do not see the fire in our earth's crust, we can appreciate its invisible warmth that, in turn, assists fertilisation. Next we see the sun at daytime, in its isolation… appearing so lonely, but mighty powerful! The sky, or air above and around us, wafts its breath in a continuous flow…awesome and unfathomable! The sea, in all its splendour and fluidic brilliance is not so distant for we can walk along the beach and paddle in its cool comfort – or bathe in it for cleanliness and freshness.

This would be our overall appreciation of a landscape, without unexpected storms, volcanoes and unpredictable circumstances.

Our star signs can become, in a general view, a beautiful landscape with Taurus, Virgo and Capricorn as the earth we see; Cancer, Scorpio and Pisces as the seas and water that so spectacularly enhance our view of the earth; Gemini, Libra and Aquarius as the refreshing balm of air that we breathe or view as the beauty of a clear blue sky; lastly,

Aries, Leo and Sagittarius as the fire and light that comfort us and lead us on our way.

Prof. Jos continued to explain to me how the earth and water mix and can turn into a useful loam to use for pottery or making bricks and other infinite usages. However to make the earth fertile there is also the need for warmth and fire such as the sun or volcanic properties, and of course, water to help with growth. Fire also needs air to maintain its power as much as earth and water require energy and aerating influences. Hence all these elements 'work together' to produce life. We all, in fact, are created and maintained by the combination of these elements. Scientists nowadays have great knowledge of this and continue to investigate ways to heal us through these essential substances.

Every star sign has a planet that exerts specific influence on a person at birth, as one would say, a blue print of the individual is created. The element that influences the planet will be the most prevalent one in the individual, but 'Fire' signs (Aries, Leo and Sagittarius) need extra consideration.

The following is a very simplified explanation to help us understand some important details about Fire Signs: - in simple terms, all matter is a combination of molecules, atoms and elements, and can exist in three states: gas, liquid or solid. Hence these three would be related to the astrological definition of AIR (Gas), WATER (Liquid), and EARTH (Solid). So, where do Aries, Leo and Sagittarius fit in, for they are FIRE signs? Although astrology simply mentions that Aries, Leo and Sagittarius have 'Fire' as their element – it is important to realize that these three signs 'need' to obtain their energy from the other nine signs because 'fire' is a combustion, or a rapid mixture of a particular element (or substance) with oxygen (air/gas) accompanied by heat or light.

This view of FIRE is very important if we are to understand Star Signs in the way Prof Jos specifically instructed me to 'observe nature' and, in so doing, to go with the flow of life on earth so as to alleviate incompatibilities, or, in any case, to have a better understanding of how to cooperate with each other for a more harmonious life on earth.

Although so much more could be said about the astrological notion of planetary elements but the purpose of this booklet is to try to explain quite complicated facts in an easy-to-read account – accessible to all who are conscious of Star Sign incompatibilities and who may need to know how the stars can help us to achieve a more harmonious existence, as long as we can understand what elements the stars have initially offered us at birth.

Chapter 4 ★★ ★ ★

VOYAGE OF DISCOVERY

During the time that Prof Jos had these conversations with me about his understanding of Star Signs my life was about to take a dramatic change. When I was eighteen years old my father died suddenly and all my dreams and aspirations for my future collapsed. Soon after I married and moved abroad. I never saw or heard of Prof. Jos again. His booklet was lost in the turmoil of moving however all his instructions were engraved in my memory forever.

At that time I did not know if all his theories would work. However, his advice to use his knowledge when I began teaching was what I endeavoured to do. In this way I would either believe in him or not.

Often I would read books on Astrology but none satisfied me –a number of them were so complicated and, in any case, how could one believe in something that even scientists would not agree on? As well as this, all the daily astrological articles in newspapers and magazines only appeared to predict the future, and this was (and is) something contrary to my own beliefs – and, above all else I had Prof. Jos's warning about the negative aspects that could be found in horoscopes - for nothing is 'fixed' in our cosmos – all is adapting and changing, according to our needs and our faith.

And so it was that I started on my voyage of discovery with my pupils. I memorised every child's date of birth and observed their character and behaviour to prove the Jos theory.

At the onset of this undertaking I did not know how and why the planets had distinct elements that in turn influenced people. However, I came to the conclusion, after more than forty years of observation and experience, that, just as there are some plants that need more water or warmth, and others that need more fresh air or a sandy soil, and so on, so do human beings need favourable elements to achieve their true potential based on each individual planetary element (i.e. fire, air, earth, water).

It was a revelation to me to begin to observe this while I was teaching. Earth signs were predictable and constant in their attempt to learn and improve their skills. Water signs would be prone to mood changes. Fire signs were liable to flare up in anger or discomfort. Air signs were in need of constant stimulation for otherwise they would become apathetic.

Although the elements of each sign were the only analytical aspect of my research, I did have to grapple with the notion that each individual also had a symbol such as The Ram, The Bull, The Twins, and so on. At first I could not accept that everyone born under a specific star sign would have the same characteristics. Added to this, each individual had a different combination of planetary positions according to their time and place of birth – so I was very perplexed. Once again I reverted to Prof Jos' guideline to 'observe nature'.

It took me a long, long time to suddenly find a simple solution. I observed the huge horse chestnut trees in my local park – they all were obviously chestnut trees, but, none was identical to each other – each and every one was quite different in colour, size and shape and yet 'of the same tree family'. This I also noticed in all living creatures...

This simple realization enabled me to accept Star signs. It did help me to observe these 'familial' characteristics in my pupils and in everyone I met.

The following is my very short version of star sign 'families':

(i)   Aries - Ram people – lively – fervent – intrepid
(Fire / Mars)

(ii) Taurus – Bull /Bovine – realistic – resolute – long-suffering
(Earth / Venus)

(iii) Gemini – Twins/All Human – adaptable – creative - enquiring
(Air / Mercury)

(iv) Cancer – Crab – caring – sensitive – instinctive
(Water / Moon)

(v) Leo – Lion / Feline – pompous – energetic – naive
(Fire / Sun)

(vi) Virgo – Human /Wheat – meticulous –
      methodical - judicious
      (Earth / Mercury)
(vii) Libra – The Scales/Object – subtle –
      calm - discreet
      (Air / Venus)
(viii) Scorpio – Dove/ Eagle/Scorpion –
      deep – seductive -emotional
      (Water / Mars / Pluto)
(ix) Sagittarius – Horse/human – confident –
      sociable - whimsical
      (Fire / Jupiter)
(x)   Capricorn – Goat – conservative –
      well-organized - go-getting
      (Earth / Saturn)
(xi) Aquarius – Human/Pot/Water –
      kind – romantic - free spirit
      (Air / Uranus)
(xii) Pisces – Two Fishes – perceptive –
      imaginative - tender
      (Water / Neptune)

In most astrology books one can find further descriptions of the nature of people born under these twelve symbols but some special points on these Star Signs are worth observing as will follow in the next chapter.

Chapter 5 ★★★★★

SPECIAL POINTS TO OBSERVE

These observations are special because they may alleviate negative aspects wrongfully attributed to some star signs. Very often we hear folk mentioning that they or someone else have traits such as the two-faced Gemini or the sting in a Scorpio tail, and so on.

The following may give us a different approach to these signs, and others, as follows:

- Gemini Star People - Gemini is the ONLY symbol (Twins) that is TOTALLY HUMAN– that is, without a symbolic animal, plant or object and not like the other signs which are: Aries / Ram; Taurus / Bull; Cancer / Crab; Leo / Lion; Virgo /human / plant; Libra / Scales / object; Sagittarius / half horse half human; Capricorn / Goat; Aquarius / human with flowing water pot; Pisces / Two Fishes; – but, NOT Gemini – no animal, object or plant is connected to this sign.

Prof Jos said that the ancient knowledge depicted the Gemini sign as 'the angelic beings' – no wonder they are quick movers and have a great deal to talk about... they may have 'two faces' but they also have two of everything! Their emotions could be said to be devoid of carnal appetites because all their experiences seem to have more of a 'heavenly-substance' than the rest in the Zodiac cycle.

- Scorpio – their symbol may be a scorpion, but some have lifted their soul from the 'hot sands of time' and have developed two new characteristics. They could be 'like a scorpion' with a sting in their tail... BUT many Scorpio symbol bearers are either like a DOVE or an EAGLE. One has to observe a Scorpio person for a short while and then a 'dove' or an 'eagle' emerges, either in outward physical appearance or in character. Some may be gentle and caring (dove-like), others are soaring to heights of goodness towards all mankind (eagle-like).

- Libra - Librans have an object as their symbol – The Balance – they may appear cold and aloof, but they need to be! This detachment from all other signs enables them to bring equilibrium to all – balancing all the Star signs… what a task! Is it not surprising then to consider that Librans may find it very difficult to 'take sides'? Could we assist them in any way? Their sense of 'fair-play' must be a daunting task for them to tackle!

- Leo - is quite unique because it is the ONLY sign that has the Sun as its ruling planet. They are lions with a special dimension amongst the other signs, because of the strong Sun influence. Hence they are so magnificent in their whole appearance– and so essential to all other living creatures! Incessantly eager to manifest their warmth and light but when their expansive nature has no one or nothing to shine upon they could even lose their will to exist.

- Aquarius – so many times I have heard Aquarians say that they are 'a water sign' because of the name derived from the Latin 'aqua' for 'water' as well as the symbol that shows 'a person dripping water from a pot'. Aquarians' element is 'AIR' and not 'water'. The water that flows from the pot is producing electricity…! They energize others but find it difficult to satisfy their own needs. Just like electricity that runs through our cables so they too are in perpetual motion searching new paths of knowledge and experience - they are perpetually upgrading…

These, therefore, are some of the points that I feel need our special attention if we are to collaborate more fully with our ever helping stars.

Chapter 6 ★ ★ ★ ★ ★

RELATIONSHIPS
AND THE STARS

Since this booklet is specifically written to help those who are already aware that their Star sign is incompatible with another (i.e. a relative, friend or business partner), the following explanations on the planetary elements and behaviour, may kindle a light of hope, knowing that at the core of every Star sign there is an important element which we are already familiar with in our every day life, such as earth, water, air and fire.

- Earth and Water Signs: Taurus, Virgo and Capricorn are Earth Signs and are compatible amongst themselves but also get along with Water Signs (Cancer, Scorpio and Pisces) - hence we observe 'nature' and notice that earth and water can produce a solid foundation

- Air and Fire Signs: Gemini, Libra and Aquarius are Air Signs and are compatible amongst themselves but they also have a good understanding with Fire Signs (Aries, Leo and Sagittarius) – nature again shows us the effective union of air and fire

In nature, however, these compatible elements can also cause devastations, such as:

- Drought (not enough water)
- Floods (earth erosion)
- Fires (too much air/wind)
- Tornadoes (hot columns of air driven by strong wind)

Therefore to really 'get on' with a 'compatible sign' one's own individual nature must be guarded – are we too possessive, or too demanding – so much so that our negative energy produces catastrophic consequences? Remember the advice: 'observe nature'… if you are an earth sign and your partner is a water sign, and if you keep filling the pond with debris, the water will seep away into a more suitable environment – pond life will die and you will be left without water to quench your thirst.

The reverse of this would be if your 'water' partner keeps 'flooding your space' with unreasonable behaviour. Water has a way of trickling on to a rock, and given time the rock is eroded…Re-route the 'drip' immediately! How? Plan extra loving chores that you know your partner loathes to do or take your partner out for a stroll, away from your environment, so that you can talk the problem over before you explode and there is an avalanche!

Similar thoughts can be attributed to Air and Fire partners. If you are an Air sign and you feel trapped by rules and regulations imposed upon by your Fire partner, then try not to 'blow your top' too often because, the fire will diminish and lose its warmth. In extreme cases the fire will increase and all around you will be destroyed. What is the simple solution? Fan the fire often with loving deeds.

The reverse of this would be if a Fire partner is constantly hot-tempered and overbearing... fire will sap up all air's energy – in such cases Air signs may become highly disturbed and may need to waft away to places where limitations are less obvious.

- These above mentioned are those considered to be 'compatible' and yet 'nature' shows us that difficulties could easily arise. So, what happens with those who have a partner who is NOT compatible and who have been troubled by the general view of incompatibilities?

These are:

- Earth Signs (Taurus/Virgo/Capricorn) and Water Signs (Pisces/Cancer/Scorpio) are known to be incompatible with Fire Signs (Aries/Leo/Sagittarius) and Air Signs (Gemini/Libra/Aquarius)

We cast our eyes again to nature and we see how the earth needs warmth to be fertile and productive and as long as there are no eruptions all will be well – if, however, there is a 'volcano' after the disruption is over the earth becomes even more productive – but this would take time, and so, it is worth remembering that a guarded temper is very necessary to maintain the partnership. Our instincts should be telling us that we are not dealing simply with a human being, but with a living being who embodies a star.

Do we not take extra care to appoint scientists and professionals to work incessantly for the good management of our world? Should we not also be like mini-scientists in our relationships too? Managing our world also means increasing our understanding of the needs of those around us so as to ever perfect our love and tenderness towards humanity.

We have mentioned 'earth and fire', but, what about 'earth and air'? In this case, Prof Jos told me that just as the earth we see in a landscape contentedly existing under the vast canopy of the sky (air), so do positive partners live a peaceful existence – maybe 'doing their own thing' but nevertheless contented and at peace.

Now we come to 'water and fire' – if we flick a little water onto a fire, the fire sparkles and brightens up… Water signs must try to be less intense with their own deep-water surges… This also applies to Fire Signs, because a large fire can extinguish water, until it evaporates. So, let us use our 'nature minds' much more and then we will be able to connect with people with an added cosmic dimension.

Finally, 'water and air' – I hope that by now you will have worked out the simple star guidance – yes, do we enjoy 'fizzy drinks'? If we do, we know how invigorating it is to drink soda drinks…or what about 'surfing' or swimming in a gentle wavy sea? What would we do without these wonderful experiences – all due to air, wind and water? I am sure that you can find many more examples of exciting ways to enjoy water and air. What about tidal waves? If they arise neither air nor water are concerned…but if the air is too gusty and the water is a gentle streamlet (by this I mean, a highly sensitive, gentle-natured Water sign person), then the waters of this stream will be tossed away into the deep surrounding cliffs and may never be seen again.

Remember, each being is linked to the stars, and each one has a unique cosmic imprint that underlies their every move. May these thoughts, based on my own discoveries after hearing Prof Jos' explanations on healing and the Stars, help many to realize that incompatibilities need not be, if we find 'nature's way' to overcome them, and if we pay close attention to our truly exceptional human capacity to love and care for one another.

Chapter 7 ★ ★ ★ ★ ★

THE ZODIAC AND CHRISTIANITY

My first glimpse into the awesome world of our 'helping stars' was the amazing discovery that the 'Wise Men' were so convinced that a unique and matchless person had been born on earth because they saw a new 'Star' formation – one which they had never seen before. They were also able to corroborate this event in ancient texts.

Many archaeologists and scientists today are in awe of the knowledge of ancient civilizations regarding the Stars – there are many books about the Egyptians and the Incas, and many other civilizations of the past, which show this. So it is not such a mystery, nowadays, that these Wise Men had star knowledge.

There are so many mysteries still waiting to be solved – the mystery of Prof Jos' theory, in my respect, is solved because of my long years of constant observation and experience in putting into practice his advice.

If the 'Wise Men' of the Bible discovered the Coming of Christ on earth because of His Star, then, should we not also be called upon to know more about 'our own star dimension'? It is wise, however, not to delve into astrological predictions and fixed ideas about our future because the power of Christ now with us on this earth has, in itself, the energy to change our very nature. We need only to stand under His beam of light and respond to His call, which is: 'I am the light of the world, he that follows me shall not walk in darkness but shall have the light of life' (St John 8:12).

Such an awesome calling! Who would want to ignore such an invitation!

It has been so important for me to add these thoughts about Jesus because I believe, just as the healing power of the stars has been lost, so has the message of Christ and His Star been, on the whole, ignored.

The light force of Christ was focussed on ALL OF US here on earth to transform our world, and us, and not for it to become a 'religion'... ('Religion' from the Latin 'religare' meaning 'to bind' humans to God – it is as if we are forever stretching out a rope to nowhere - Christ's light is shed for us just like our sun shines for us – we can choose to draw the curtains and eliminate its light – but, it is still shining, regardless of what we say and do...)

Just think for a moment! Our very own Star signs can direct us to the most important star of all, The Star of Bethlehem! The knowledge derived from this Star will help us prepare our bodies for our new life – in a home within the stars where God shall wipe away all tears from our eyes; 'and there will be no more death, neither sorrow, nor crying, neither shall there be any more pain: for the former things are passed away' (Rev 21:4).

This is awesome! This is not religion – it is cosmic wonder!

Those Magi knew an astronomical event when they saw one and realized that our planet earth and we would never be the same again!

About the Author

Ariane Warren has written this book after forty years of observing the influence of the elements of Star Signs (Fire, Earth, Water and Air) in her pupils and colleagues. Her teaching career enabled her to corroborate her mentor's advice - advice that he gave her in 1966 – especially regarding Star Sign incompatibilities.

Many folk who have benefited from her advice have asked her to write a book about her findings. Now, at last, she has completed her easy guide to understand Star Signs and fervently hopes that it will help those who feel trapped by the notion that some Star Signs are incompatible with their own astrological birth sign.

The book has been specifically written in an 'easy-to-read' manner especially dedicated to those who are busy amongst the hustle and bustle of life but who would be relieved to know that there is nothing to fear concerning Star Sign incompatibilities – our 'nature-elements' hold the key…!

Her teaching subject was Music in Education and taught Primary and Secondary Mainstream Classes – in her latter years she specialised in Pupils with Additional Needs. Her main musical instrument is the piano. She gained a Licentiate of the Trinity College of Music in London in 1978 as well as two Alberto Williams Conservatoire Music Diplomas in Piano and Theory of Music in Buenos Aires.

She has obtained Merits of Excellence for her work in the British Government Educational System. Throughout the past forty years she has written many dramatic works for stage and musical performances. One of these has been published entitled 'Prince of Peace'.

The Author hopes to continue publishing her life-long experiences so that she may encourage and comfort many midst adversity and confusion.

Even though Ariane Warren prefers to remain anonymous, her real name and proof of her credentials are available for verification from her publishers.